Dese Shoes

And Other Poems

Loretta (Firekeeper) Hawkins

Copyright © 2017 Loretta A. Hawkins

All rights reserved.

ISBN-13: 978-0692952511 (Firekeeper Artistry)

ISBN-10: 0692952519

v

DEDICATION

 Dese Shoes, especially, and the other poems in this book are dedicated to all the women I've loved before. All of the women who have been a cognizant presence in my existence. All of the women who came before: my ancestors; all those who breathe freely now, my contemporaries, and all those who will come after, my descendants. If it is true, as I believe, that we are created in the image of God, I dedicate this work to Her, for my very presence and for Her mercy and kindness toward me.

 I give homage to my grandmothers, Mable Self, maternally, and Ida Sanders, my father's mother, both of whom worked from childhood to death to ensure that our generations continued. I thank my mother, Laurine (Blink) Hines Sanders, whom I can never forget, and will always remember as the most influential presence in my life. She built the bridge that I crossed over on. She was the first woman that I knew personally, that I ever loved. I thank her sisters, my aunts Jeanette, Virginia, Connie Mae and Stella who brought love and laughter into my life. I thank my sister, Wanda Long who has been by my side, since forever.

 I thank the women to whom I have given birth, my daughters: Robin, my firstborn; Dionne, my middle child, and Sherri, my baby. When I reflect on how wonderful they are, and have always been, it brings tears to my eyes. My love for them is eternal. I thank my granddaughters, Arieyanna and Cheyenne, for I prayed to God to allow me to live long enough to see their faces. These are all my children. I thank god into the future for my children yet unborn.

 When I think of all the women I have met and loved these many years, there are thousands!! They are my cousins, my childhood friends, my adult and life-long friends, my fellow students, my own students, my fellow poets, young and old, and my friends today who have supported me in my artistic endeavors.

 Finally, I dedicate this book to Harriet Tubman, my personal historical shero. I loved her before I ever knew she existed. I am grateful for all she did and all she was. She freed me!! My next book of poetry will be dedicated to all the men I've loved before, and there are many. But this book here? This book's for you, Harriet !!

All rights reserved. No part of this publication may be reproduced or transmitted in any form or by any means, electronic or mechanical, including photocopy, recording, or any information storage and retrieval system, without permission in writing from the publisher.
Requests for permission to make copies of any part of this work should be emailed to:
firekeeperartistry@gmail.com

Library of Congress Cataloging in Publication Data
Hawkins, Loretta
Dese Shoes
ISBN-13: 978-0692952511
ISBN-10: 0692952519

Printed in the United States of America
Copyright November 2, 2016 by Loretta A. Hawkins

CONTENTS

DESE SHOES	1
WHITE EYES	9
AND OUR SPIRITS HAVE NOT BEEN BROKEN	12
MZCONCEPTION	34
ONE LITTLE THING	36

ACKNOWLEDGMENTS

I wish to thank Jerode (Jeronimo) Rodgers and Alicia Restore Spikes for all they did in making the publication of this book a success. From finding images for the book cover, graphic designing, to networking with the formatter, they both were always available, willing and able to help move the project forward.

Special thanks to Jasmine Cummings, for all she did to perfect the images to the template, and to ensure that the interior of the book was properly inserted. Many hours were spent assuring that all was as it should be. I appreciate all the time you expended to acquire perfection.

Thanking my daughters, Robin, Dionne, and Sherri for all they did and all they provided, to help.

Last, but not least, thanking God.

*"Just like moons and like suns
With the certainty of tides
Just like hopes springing high
Still I'll rise."*

~ Maya Angelou

FIREKEEPER ARTISTRY

Chicago , Illinois

DESE SHOES

Chil'ren, my name is Harriet. Some of y'all don't know much about me, I bet. Cause they don't teach much history in these modern- days schools. Look at dese shoes. Bout wore out, the leather almost gone. But, I can still sing a song. Cause dese shoes done took me where I wanted to be. Dese shoes walked me to free!

I was born on a plantation in Maryland. My master, Master Brodus, was mean to me. From a child on up, he did things to me. That made me ashamed of me. But I was a slave child, what could I do? I promised myself, I gon get way from you. If it's the last thing on this earth I ever do.

Look here. See that lil hole right there in my shoe? That's where Master Brodus took a nail, and hammered it through. Through my shoe, through my foot, and clean through the sole. That was my punishment for breaking that lil bowl.

One day he took a big, old piece of lead, and because I was too slow, he hit me on the head. Everybody thought I was just plain old dead. Cause I went into a deep, dark sleep. They say I slept for more than a week. My mama sat by my side at night, and she would weep, and I would sleep. And I would sleep.

After that, I'd have these mysterious spells. Where I would just fall asleep and nobody could tell, if I was alive or if I was dead. Cause they couldn't wake me up for three or four hours, they said. Then suddenly I'd just open my eyes and smile. And most of this happened while I still was a child.

I had to wait til I was bout twenty-fo', when I knew I couldn't take slavery not another day mo. I knew if I stayed in Maryland, I would die. So I had to escape. I had to try! But it wasn't easy. There was slave - catcher men, roaming all over the state, way back then. And if they caught you running away, you might not live to *see* another day.

And if you *did* live – you sometimes wish you had died. I seen them throw a run-a-way into a big ol' pot of hot oil and cooked him til he fried. Back then, they whipped us hanging from a tree. And they wouldn't stop whipping til they could see, our flesh hanging free, from our bones.

We had no homes – we slept in a shack. – so many in one, we was almost stacked – on top of each other, like sardines in a can. I never regretted that day that I ran. I ran in dese shoes – no such thang as a car. I ran in dese shoes. I ran so far. I ran from Maryland, from slavery! I ran for my life, so it could be free.

Sometimes - I look down, from heaven, up high. And every time I look, I start to cry.

Cause I see that y'all still running too. The savages is still savages- they still killing you. And I pray for you. I pray for you!

One day I asked God if I could come down. She looked at me – gave a slight kind of frown. She asked why I wanted to come down. Cause down here I be earthly – in these wore –out shoes – in this raggedy old gown. She said, up here, in the spirit, you are divine!

"Up here you have wings and you can fly. Down there you're almost crippled and you are old. Down there you have them shoes with a hole in the sole. Up here, you'll be safe by my side. Down there – you'll be controlled by racist lies!"

But I told God, "I need to go there. Where my people is suffering, and God, I swear, on all that is dear to me: I'll just stay one day: so here I be. Chil'ren, I come here today to talk to you. To try to tell you what you ought to do. To tell you what in slavery, we *had* to do. So that our then unborn would become the now you. And how the hope of the slave created a new way, for you. And how our people survived slavery and we came through!

After I got free, somebody ask me, "Do you believe in hell?" I told them certainly I do. I was born there. I was raised there! That's where all us slaves dwelled! Yeah, we *lived* in hell, and there was more devils than sin. And all them wrapped up in fine clothes and white skin!

After I got free, I wasn't satisfied. All I did was sat round and cried. Cause my mama, my daddy, my sisters, my bro. Although still alive, was still in slavery though. So I had to go back, to set them free. I wanted my family to be free like me. But it wasn't a easy thang, though.

After freeing my family, I made many trips mo , using the Underground Railroad and they life-saving tips. We learned to walk crouched down- so we wouldn't get hit. To keep they feets from freezing, they'd step in horse dung, but they couldn't stand there too long cause we'd get caught and get hung. We looked to the heavens, following the North Star. Cause like I said before, no such thang as a car.

We rubbed the bark of trees, feeling for moss. And that's how we kept our-selfs from getting too lost. We'd come to rivers, filled with alligators – a poisonous snake! But these were the rivers we had to take. We'd walk straight in, carrying the hope that faith makes. Some people would grow weary, and would want to go back. I told them naw, we won't give up - and we won't back- track. I told them , Naw, you gon be free, or you gon be dead. And I have this gun to make sure. Yeah, that's what I said. I said, naw! We gon be free! We gon be free! Whether dead or alive – that's the way it gon be.

One old man came up to me, said, "Harriett, "I'm too old. I'm too tired. I just can't go on." I said, " then that spot where you stand will be your permanent home." And I meant that thang, chil' ren. I meant that thang.

Cause if he went back, that meant we all would hang. I said nobody's going back!! Nobody's going back!! Y'all all gotta try. Everybody!! Cause the spot where you give up – will be the spot where you die!!

I made many trips – never had to dig any graves. And could have freed so many more, if only they knew they were slaves. So child'ren, I want you to remember and see, that that thang they called freedom – It never was free. I thank God, Almighty for dese shoes on my feet, cause most slaves didn't have shoes, they walked through they life barefeet.

Now I'm getting to the part that I came here to say, cause I don't know if God will let me come back another day. Chil'ren. You got to change your ways. Look back at how we done in them slavery days. Now, I know y'all thinking, oh, she want us to be like the slaves? Before we do that, we'll stomp on our own mama's graves!!

But I say, yes, yes! I want you to be like the slave. Cause the slave was not cowardly – in fact the slave was brave. How easy it would have been to fall on the sword, especially if you thought heaven would be your reward. A more courageous thang the slave did was to refuse to die. In spite of the atrocities - he said I got to try to live in spite of them I scorn - I got to live for my yet unborn.

So all you young chil'ren out there, listen to me, if you want to be a parent eventually. If you're walking down the street on a summer day, police stop you, for no reason, do what they say! They mostly want to hurt your feelings – make you feel bad. They want to call you nigger. Want to make you mad. So take the insult, like our ancestors did. That's better than laying beneath a coffin's lid!

Our ancestors were not cowards. They played low to them they scorn. They took that dung, buried it, so you could be born! You take it too from them you scorn. You take it too, for your yet unborn. That's what I did til I could find a better way. And until that day come, map out your plans, of what you will do to make a better day.

Chil'ren, you still continue to unjustly die. And you do not understand the reason why. It's because you are the unorganized truth, fighting against the organized lie. You are the dream of the slave that some let the dream die. You are a people who done been whipped til they forgot who they be. For this one moment is time, done forgot our glorius history.

Another thang I need to say before I be through – and this is just to the lost souls out there – What's wrong with you?!! I know from history that some oppressed people imitate they oppressors – try to do like they do. – so now some of y'all out there shooting and killing us, too. What's wrong with you?!! Haven't the oppressors killed – still is killing enough of you – that you got to join in and help them kill us, too? What's wrong with you?!! You pitiful ! You lost yoself!! You lost in them woods – can't find your way through!!

When I look down and I see you, I be ashamed - ashamed of you!! But I still, I still, I still pray for you.

Back then they did everything bad they could think of - to us. Cut off a finger –cut off a toe. But y'all showed them who we be in 2016 – Rio. Showed we run faster, we hit harder, we even can swim – In boxing, in basketball, we win on a whim. Our melanin is showing the world who we be. Showed the world what is meant by true dominance, you see.

We were the first people and we will be the last. How this future knowledge did I come to see? Turns out God is a black female, like me. She told me remember when, as a child, you slept for a week? I was planting the knowledge of how to escape in your sleep. I was planting the memory of the route in your brain, injecting you with stamina so the journeys would not be a strain.

I was fortifying your courage so you would not be afraid. Showing you how to hide them shoes and that gun, in case of a raid. I was preparing you. You called it a plan, having not the slightest idea in was all in my hand.

Remember on your journeys, you would sometimes have a lil spell? That's cause there was danger nearby and I'd have to tell you which way to go, now. Which way was safe. While you slept I'd make you remember a new route - there could be no mistakes and there could be no doubt. You had to learn each new road, each new tree. So that when you woke up, your third eye would and could see.

So Unify! Organize, my chil'ren. Make plans ! Then manifest your destiny cause it's all in God's hands. Above all make sure you live - to fight in the struggle another day. You chil,ren must forge another way. Remember to not foolishly die! Until it's your time, of course. So chil'ren , try. I love you, my people and I would have died for you!! And now, from up above, whatever I do, I promise you, chil'ren, I still pray for you!!

This evil from savages will not last. Racism will one day be a thang of the past. It has been written that the last shall be first and the first shall be last. I further proclaim that it will be ,that the first shall be last and the last shall be free. Remember me, and remember dese shoes. Oh, mighty, Black people !! There's no way we can lose !!

White Eyes

I once wrote a poem , entitled 1933, wherein I painted a vivid portrait of exactly how it might be, to be a black American, hanging from a tree ! Today the year is AD – 2017, I think of all the years that's passed – the Jim Crow years between, and try to phantom exactly, what all that suffering means. And close my ears to obliterate memories of silent screams.

When I think of that old poem, written in the clear ink of my tears - when I think of my humble people and all those death-filled years, I realize reality is not always as it appears. When they were killing us in America in 1933, there was one strange phenomenon that was always a mystery to me: When they killed an innocent black person, and their eyes were filled with glee - I wondered God in Heaven! Can white eyes really see?!! Can white eyes see true injustice? Can white eyes see human pain? Can white eyes internalize what they see? Or are white eyes just insane?

I think of the eyes that saw Jesus Christ, hanging from a cross. The eyes that dragged Freddie Gray, but could not see human loss. The eyes that could not see Tamir Rice was a child playing in the park – could not see he was just a little boy - although it was not even dark.

Today, as I said before, is 2017. Today white eyes are scanning a city street – they're at a murder scene. A black boy is lying face -down dead – a bullet in his back. But the white eyes that are reporting say that he was the one who attacked. And when the white eyes that are reporting lie – than that becomes the fact.

But it is not the white eyes that are reporting that I fear – the eyes that give me pause. No, it is the white eyes that are listening that I fear the most because – the white eyes that are listening, those white eyes belong to you. And your white eyes feel in your benevolence, your moral vision is true. But if your white eyes are not insane, wouldn't they see what is actually true?

And if your eyes would see what is true – you have the power to --- Oh, let me stop! I hope to deep! My hopes are bound to make me weep. Perhaps white eyes are not insane. Perhaps white eyes are just asleep.

Some white eyes are awake and wise - like the eyes of Jane Elliott and Timothy Wise! They see with a clarity that's beyond human guise. I wish we all had their six eyes. Their eyes see so deep, they make me weep. Their sheer humanity makes me cry. Their eyes would not have allowed anyone to prematurely die. Not Jesus Christ or Tamir Rice ! Not Dr. King or Freddie Gray ! Not Joan of Arc or Sandra Bland!

Not Abraham Lincoln, or George Mann ! There are many white eyes that are open and bold. White eyes that saw and built an Underground railroad! White eyes that died with John Brown and his sons. And white eyes that rode on Freedom buses that were bombed!

But the white eyes that can see are the minority ! And the white eyes that are blind are the majority! And until those two facts become diametrically reversed -- God help white eyes - and God help us!!

And Our Spirits Have Not Been Broken

"In the beginning, God created the heaven and the Earth."
And five days later, he created us, the African People.
We are the Alpha and the Omega. The Alpha of Mankind.
We are the first people of this planet.
We are the first Humans of Earth.
We are the original Homo Sapiens.
Human life on this planet was created, through us, with us, for us.
We are the indomitable ones.
And our spirits have not been broken.
Our earthly lives are but a token
Of God's mercy and kindness towards us.
We are the indomitable ones,
With souls that are unconquerable.
In the Beginning, we were created by God
Who tenderly rocked us - in the cradle of civilization ,
Wherein He indubitably showed his kindness towards us.
We were created by God, at the dawn of civilization,
And placed in a garden east in Eden,
In a place that would come to be known as Africa.
Rising up out of the dust of Africa
We spread our seeds throughout the continent.
And then throughout the continents
Before the land separated from itself

And thus became separated by oceans and seas.
We were created by God as free beings.
To hold domination over the land and over the seas
And over every beast and fowl that God created.
Then, we were born free.
And as man and woman, and as determined by God,
 Chosen to rule the Earth.
The ancient Ethiopians named themselves the Anu,
Later to be called, Ethiopian, or "burnt face" by the ancient Greek.
The ancient Egyptians named their land Khem,
Or Kemit, which means "land of the blacks."
These peoples, our ancestors
 were the creators of painting, sculpture, architecture,
The calendar, astrology, the pyramids, hieroglyphics,
 And of all human civilization.
 Mummified kings, queens, and pharaohs were preserved
 Inside opulently adorned golden sarcophagus'
Lying deeply inside pyramids,
Centuries before ancient Rome or ancient Greece
Came into existence.
The Great Pyramid of Khufu had already stood for 1800 years
Before the Chinese laid the first stone into
The Great Wall of China.
Chamber walls of hieroglyphics
 Adorned with rubies and gold
Told a tale of our people and
Our magnificence,
Long before the Rosetta Stone
Opened its lips to reveal the truth.

We were created by God as: Wolof, Temne, Mende, Vai, Gola
Bambara, Mandingo, Ewe, Ebo, Fante, Ashante,
Luba, Fulani, Tuareg, Ga, Kisi, Ovimbundu,
And so forth and so on,
And our spirits have not been broken.
Our earthly lives were but a token.
We were re-created – by the white man's greed.
We are the unintended consequence of that insatiable cupidity.
For after a forced trek from inland Africa to the shores,
Bare-footed, naked, and half naked, chained and afraid
The weak died off.
When our captured ancestors reached the awaiting ship
Only the strongest of Africa walked aboard.
Indomitably.
But our spirits were not broken
Our earthly lives a mere token
Of God's mercy and kindness towards us.
The Middle Passage! That historic, horrific hell on God's sea
Tightly packed into a ship's hell-hull for months
Lying and sliding on rough, splintered floor- boards.
Being urinated upon all day by the person lying chained, behind you,
And being defecated upon at night
 by the person chained to the front of you.
And you, involuntarily reciprocating in turn,
Gagging, grasping for air, putrid and toxic
From the combined odors of urine, vomit, feces, blood, semen and pus.
Hosed down, male and female, to be raped by the savage captors.

Disease and death reigned.
Again, the weak died off.
Some were finally free, unchained and thrown overboard
To become food for the sharks whose habit it became
To follow slave ships.
Day, after horrific day – chained to one another's misery.
Yet our spirits were not broken
Our earthly lives were a mere token
Of God's mercy and kindness to us.
When the lighter ship, after a seemingly eternity,
reached the shores of North, Central, South America
And the islands of the Caribbean
Only the strongest *of the strongest*
Of Africa walked ashore,
Indomitably.
Reclassified, no longer were we man or woman, or child,
But slave, for we were now in America.
But our spirits were not broken.
Our pitiful lives merely a token
Of God's mercy and kindness to us.
Cupidity of the savages, led them to force breed us, tribe with tribe.
And so we were bred, like animals, tribe with tribe:
The strongest of the Mandingos, with the strongest of the Mende.
The most intelligent of the Goree with the most resourceful of the Ewe.
The most creative of the Tucolor with the genius of the Songhai,

The magnificent physiques of the Dinkas, the "men of men"
With the beauty of the Wodaabe men.
And so forth and so on.
By the time the forced breeding of tribes ended,
Which was when slavery ended,
We, as a people, possessed the greatest strength,
Adaptability, intelligence, creativity, inventiveness,
Ingenuity, genius, physicality, and resourcefulness
that Africa had to offer.
And our earthly lives were but a token
And our spirits were not broken.
And for four hundred years, slavery reigned.
We slaved. Without us realizing it,
Not internalizing the reality of it all.
But when we think about slavery,
A time that use to be,
We think of our people
And so clearly we see
We were brought to this country
To be the animals of whites
With no thoughts of humanity, with no human rights
Of all the atrocities in history of things done to us
Only one thing was done to animals
that was not done to us.
We were bought just like cattle
We were sold just like swine
We were branded with fire
From pure white, hot iron
We were bred just like horses
We were raped by slave masters ,
And the children we bore
Were by the owners called bastards.

Of all the atrocities in history, of things done to us
Only one thing was done to animals
 that was not done to us.
We were hanged from the trees,
Whipped until black backs ran red.
While our children watched forcefully
So they too, would be afraid.
We slaved sun up to sun down
 And If short, mutilations.
To control sexual desire,
Black men knew castrations.
Of all the atrocities in history
Of things done to us
Only one thing was done to animals
That was not done to us.
Only *one* thing was done to animals
That was not done to us
We thank a Merciful God Almighty
That they didn't -- eat us.
And our spirits were not broken
For our lives were mere tokens
Of God's mercy and kindness to us.
And so slavery endured.
Generation after generation,
We survived. We lived.   We even thrived.
For we are the indomitable ones.
Unlike whites who were forced into unpaid labor,
But died off, almost immediately,
From weakness.
Unlike Native Americans who were
Forced into unpaid labor.
But committed suicide,

Almost annihilated by their own principles.
We – we became the craftsmen of the land
We learned quickly, we adapted easily.
We improvised. We invented.
We became the builders, the ironsmiths,
The carpenters, the architects.
We built magnificent mansions
On the plantations of the South,
Built the White House in
Washington, D.C.
Designed the architectural layout of that capital city.
Built court- houses and city halls
In towns and cities throughout the land.
We built bridges and railroads
Miles and miles of track,
Without pay or compensation
But our spirits were not broken
Our lives a true token
Of God's mercy and kindness towards us.
And some of us learned to read
In spite of laws prohibiting it.
And some of us learned to write,
In spite of threats of death.
And some of us found, that in a country where
There was no place to run and no place to hide
That, in God's mercy, there existed such a place
And we were shown the way there
By people like, our Moses, Harriet Tubman
And other conductors of
The Underground Railroad
And we were hidden there, from the savages
By people like Thomas Garrett, William Still, Jarm Loguen,

William Lloyd Garrison, Amelia Bloomer,
And other, countless, nameless white men,
And white women - risking their own safe, white lives
In order to obtain freedom for slaves unknown to them,
Whom they had never seen before
and would never see again.
And our spirits remained unbroken.
For God's mercy had now spoken.
For there were those who fought for us
When we had no weapons with which to fight.
People like John Brown and his sons
And our freedom became their cause for existence.
A fact proven at Harper's Ferry in 1859
Where Brown, with eighteen men were seized.
Ten men were killed, two of them Brown's sons.
John Brown was hanged by the United States government
In December, 1859. His crime:
Attempting to set free, children of God.
And because to these freedom-fighters, God had spoken,
Our spirits were still not broken.
And six years later, after the massacre at Harper's
Ferry, The physical chains were broken.

Then out of the darkness that covered us
We became free again.
Free at last! Free at last!
Thank God Almighty! We were free at last!
One old slave, of the four million freed said,
"We ain't what we wanna be, and we ain't what we oughta be.

But thank God Almighty, we ain't what we use to be."
A civil war had been waged,
And Freedom had won
And with our spirits still unbroken,
And the horrid chains now broken
The miraculous words were spoken: You are free!
And so slavery ended - and the Black Codes began.
The Black Codes! Laws written just for us.
Written to inform us of what we could not do,
Now that we were free.
Mississippi Black Codes, the first to be passed.
The Emancipation Proclamation was written in 1865.
The Mississippi Black Codes Law were written in 1865,
The same year, to be effective beginning one year later.
The Mississippi Black Codes Law, The Vagrancy Law
A model swiftly followed by similar laws passed
In every former slave state.

Mississippi Black Codes Vagrancy Law: (It was written,) (that all freedmen, free negroes and mulattoes in this State, over the age of eighteen years, found on the second Monday in January, 1866, or thereafter, without lawful employment or business, or found unlawfully assembling themselves together, either in the day or night time…shall be deemed vagrants, (arrested) and fined in a sum not exceeding fifty dollars

and imprisoned.)

It is important to remember that slaves
were freed penniless and did not have fifty dollars

to pay a fine because he or she did not have a job.
How evil is it to enslave people for all of their lives,
Free them, then arrest them a year later for not having a job!
But our spirits were not broken,
But our spirits were not broken.
Blacks learned in the year of emancipation, that
One year later, and every year thereafter,
All Blacks, ages eighteen to eighty must pay
A tax of one dollar yearly for
Being black or they would be arrested.
Children *under* the age of eighteen,
Many of whom had been sold away
From their parents during slavery,
Were taken into the "custody of the state"
If they could not produce parents
who could support them financially.
And there were tens of thousands
Of such children,
Who did not know where their parents were
Or even who their parents were.
These children were apprenticed to their former owners
Until they became adults.
These former owners were
Referred to as "masters" in the written laws – post slavery.
The masters were allowed to discipline the children
With corporal punishment.
Any child who ran away,
If recaptured, was arrested.
Under the Mississippi Black Codes
Vagrancy Laws : if you were black,

You could not walk beside a railroad track,
Or you would be arrested.
You could not talk loudly in public,
Or you would be arrested
You could not testify against a white person
In a court of law,
Or you would be arrested
You could not allow your house to be unclean
Or you would be arrested.
Unless you were in the army,
You could not carry a gun,
Or Bowie knife,
Or you would be arrested.
You could not be drunk in public,
Or you would be arrested.
Black men must remove their hats
In the presence of a white person,
Or you would be arrested.
Once employed, you could not quit
Your job, without permission
From your white employer
Or you would be arrested,
And, if arrested for quitting your job,
you must return all money that was earned
From that employer that year.
You could not spend your earned money foolishly,
Or you would be arrested.
You could not be disrespectful to a white person,
Or you would be arrested.
You could not be homeless,
Or you would be arrested
You could not own property,
Or you would be arrested,

You could not rent land outside of the city limits
Or you would be arrested.
(If you rented land outside of the city,
because you knew how to farm,
You might be able to earn money,
So "no, " you could not rent land outside of the city limits.)
It was one of hundreds of laws,
 that applied only to black people.
You could not vote.
You could not be a judge.
You could not be a lawyer.
You could not sit on a jury.
You could not marry a white person.
You could not live in a dwelling
"on terms of equality"
With a white person
You could not be homeless.
Violation of any of these crimes
Would dictate you be arrested,
Imprisoned, and fined.
But our spirits were not broken.
Our earthly presence but a token
Of God's mercy and kindness towards us.
All of these laws, these Black Codes
Would begin in 1866, one year after the signing
Of the Emancipation Proclamation.
And just as promised, one year later
In 1866, the massive arrests began.
We were arrested by the tens.
We were arrested by the hundreds.
We were arrested by the thousands.

We were arrested by the tens of thousands.
We were arrested by the millions.
But our spirits were not broken.
Lord, our spirits were not broken!
But arrest did not mean you sat in a jail.
Arrest meant you were fined.
These were fines against people who
Had worked all of their lives, as slaves,
And had never received a penny for their labor,
And were then freed penniless.
They had no money to pay a fine.
Many freedmen returned to their
Former plantations and begged
Their former slave masters for employment
To avoid going to jail or prison.
Many plantation owners
Allowed them to return,
But would pay them in food and shelter only.
Many freedmen accepted the offer,
Since nowhere were they going to be paid
Much money anyway.
After all, after slavery, the South
was now flooded with four million
Freed Black people, desperately seeking employment.
And if the second Monday of January came,
And you had no written contract of employment,
You were going to be arrested and sent to prison, anyway.
But our spirits were not broken.
But our spirits were not broken.
Once arrested, you must pay a fine,
Which paid the arresting sheriff five dollars
And the clerk two dollars

And the white witness two dollars.
Indeed, some poor whites became
Professional witnesses, lying to the
Sheriff that they saw you walking beside
a railroad track, which for you,
was a criminal offense.
After all, you could not dispute the witness in a court,
For he or she was white,
And black people could not, by law, dispute a white person's word.
Since only white people could be witnesses,
You could not testify against him or her,
Or you were charged a second time
 and your fine increased.
Imagine nine dollars in fines
Because a white person said he saw you
Walking beside a railroad track
When you were in fact, inside your house
Cleaning it so that you would not be arrested
For having an unclean house.
Or you were engaged in any number of activities
To avoid arrest.
Nine dollars! More money than you had ever had
At any one time in your entire life.
More money than you earned in a year,
If you had a job.
If arrested and you had no money to pay your fine,
Any white person could pay your fine for you.
Especially your former slave owner.
To repay that person, you were required
 to go with him or her, and work off the fine
by working for the fine-payer, without pay.

And so slavery by another name began.
And we were taken from the jails and prisons
By the thousands and millions.
We were taken back to the plantations.
Taken to the farms.
Taken to the factories.
Taken to the coal mines.
Taken to the quarries
And the railroads.
Taken into homes
And shacks
To be worked
Or raped,
Or tortured
Or murdered
Or for whatever reason suited one's fancy,
For once a person paid your fine,
You belonged to them for a
Court-ordered amount of time.
We were taken wherever a white person
 wanted to take us
And do whatever a white person
Wanted us to do.
Or we were arrested and fined.
Yet our spirits remained unbroken.
For our lives were still a token
Of God's mercy.
We see ourselves in old black and white movies,
Wearing black and white stripped suits,
 Chained – to a gang of hundreds
Of other black men
And women. Breaking rocks,
While being guarded by white men

Sitting on horses, and later,
 In pick-up trucks, with guns.
And we wonder, as we view our criminal selves,
In such large numbers, on the silver screen.
Are Black people born criminals?
Are we innately bad?
For we are unaware that
This was the man- created source of
The criminalization of black people.
Ninety percent of those prisoners
That we saw on the chain gang
In the movies
Were arrested for vagrancy,
Not murder, or bank robbery, or
Anything violent.
 So our spirits are not broken.
No, our spirits are not broken.
And we love our brothers and sisters still.
This practice of black people as slave-prisoners
Lasted in the United States until World War II.
And then the Black Codes,
Which had originally been named The Slave Codes
Were re-named again and modified.
They became known as Jim Crow Laws.
And now we could not sit on the front of a bus,
Although we paid the same fare as every white passenger,
And if the seats in the front of the bus filled up,
We were required, by law
To remove ourselves from our seat in the
Colored section of the bus,
And give our seat to any white person standing

For they should not possibly stand, if your black self was sitting,
Because they were white and superior.
If you refused to give up your seat
So a white person could sit,
You would be arrested.
And we could not drink from a water fountain labeled
"White Only," or we would be arrested.
And we could not sit at a lunch counter,
Or we would be arrested.
We could not use a public toilet
At a bus station,
Or we would be arrested.
Or walk or sit in a public park,
Or a public swimming pool
Or a public library,
Or a public courthouse,
Although we paid the same taxes as a white person,
Or we would be arrested.
We could not go into restaurants,
Or movie houses – except in the balcony
Or any place in America that was deemed
Decent, or wonderful, or American.
America, we learned, was to be enjoyed by
White people only
In spite of the "and justice for all proclamation lie."
 And then Emmitt Till came, and Rosa Parks came,
And Martin Luther King, Jr. came.
And there were struggles of massive proportions
There were police dogs, and whips,
And water hoses, and cattle prods, and billy clubs.
And again we were arrested by the thousands.
And our bodies filled the jails and the prisons.

But our spirits were not broken.
Dr. King was arrested for telling us
To not ride the segregated buses.
From behind bars he demanded us,
"Keep walking! Keep walking!"
Just as Harriett Tubman had demanded
Her escaped runaways
A century earlier.
And so we walked.
Along long dusty dirt roads,
Along small- city streets
In sweltering heat and bitter cold
Mile after defiant mile.
And our white brothers and sisters
Who truly believed in the Fatherhood of God,
And the brotherhood of man
Went to jail with us
Were water-hosed with us,
Were whipped with us,
Were shot with us,
 Were beaten unconscious with us.
Died with us
Died for us.
 And our spirits were not broken.
White people, and people
Of all colors and religions joined us.
Walked hand in hand with us across the
Edmund Pettis Bridge as we tried, for a third time to
Walk from Selma to Montgomery.
 But our spirits were not broken.
A cosmic Spirit had now spoken.
And that is when we learned, as a people

That courage is not doing a thing and being unafraid;
Courage is doing a thing in spite of being afraid.
And our ancestors' courage carried them across that bridge.
And those brave souls, of every color, religion, nationality
And creed, became the Bridge that we,
Who could not be there,
And the unborn generations to come, crossed over on.
So after Emmitt came,
And Rosa came,
And Martin came,
We overcame.
And so a new world order of society began in America.
In America. A Civil Rights Law was passed.
The lynchings diminished, then stopped.
The schools were desegregated.
The busses and movie theaters were integrated.
And white people began to
Stop denouncing,
And began embracing
Black music, black dance and black culture.
And others began to appreciate
The evolution of black music:
The slave songs, folk music, gospel, blues, Rock and Roll, Jazz,
And others began to acknowledge
The superior athleticism of Black people, and admitted that
The Jackie Robinsons and Ernie Banks had had to endure racist abuse
In order to demonstrate that we
Had the spirit and the strength to take *any* sport to a

new level.
The world had never before seen the
Likes of a Jackie Robinson, a Jesse Owens
Or a John A. Johnson, a Joe Lewis, a Leroy Satchel Paige,
A Wilma Rudolph, a Wilt Chamberlain, or a Muhammad Ali.
Indeed, for centuries, America had refused to allow Blacks
To compete in professional sports.
Was it a secret fear that if allowed, blacks would dominate
In boxing, in football, basketball, golf, tennis and track?
Like Muhammad Ali did, and Walter Payton did
 and Michael Jordon did, or Tiger Woods did,
Or Serena Williams does, or Usain Bolt does
And in music today, every music genre created
In the United States, with the exception of
Country and Western,
Were created by African-Americans.
And African-Americans invented in number unprecedented:
Garrett A. Morgan invented the gas mask and the traffic signal.
Lewis H. Latimer invented the electric lamp,
Grandville T. Woods invented the Railway Telegraph,
Jan Matzeliger invented the shoe lasting machine,
J.A. Johnson invented the wrench,
Dr. George F. Grant invented the golf tee,
Sarah Boone invented the ironing board.
Patricia E. Bath was the first woman doctor to patent a medical invention:

A method for removing cataracts.
And in medicine, an African –American doctor,
Dr. Daniel Hale- Williams, was the
First to perform open-heart surgery,
And the patient lived.
And another doctor, Dr. Benjamin S. Carson, was the
First neurosurgeon to successfully
Separate conjoined twins at the head.
Yet another, Dr. Charles Drew,
 was the first doctor to create a blood plasma bank.
Black inventors out- performed.
Black inventors invented disproportionately
To our numbers.
And a new peace was forged.
And a long awaited calm settled over the land.
But as Dr. Julia Hare
So eloquently surmised,
"Integration merely gave the illusion of inclusion."
We are guilty of believing a lie.
We were told two powerful lies for centuries.
The first lie we were taught is that because we are black,
We are a minority. And we believed it.
Yet history illustrates that when the Europeans sailed to foreign shores,
Every spot on Earth where their ships landed,
The Europeans found people of color.
The peoples of the earth are colored people.
Black, brown, red, yellow.
Only in Europe were people white.
Therefore white people are the true minority among humans.
They are ten percent of the human population.

People of color are ninety percent of the human population.
The second lie we were taught was that white people are superior.
Genetically.
Science clearly illustrated the untruth of that fallacy.
Science shows us that white genes are recessive.
Black genes are dominant.
The mixture of the two will invariably produce
A person of color. A colored person.
And therein lies the cause of racism.
Mixture of the two races will eventually
annihilate the race of people who identify themselves as white.
The fact of the matter is that we, people or color, are a majority.
And today mitochondria DNA evidence
Shows proof positive that all humans
On the face of this planet,
Are the descendants of African people.
We are the Alpha, and for so many reasons, we will be
The Omega.

MZCONCEPTIONS
(IN LOVING MEMORY OF CONNIE JONES)

There is a grave misconception about what happened last Friday night. So I went to Connie's poem, "I Am," to illustrate that perhaps I'm right. Some people seem to think she's gone. They think that she's passed away. But reading her poem, "I Am" made me think about this a different way.

She said, "I am the image of truth and I am destiny." And truth and destiny never die. They can always only be. She said I am the expectation of some, but much more than you see." We saw a woman shroud in beauty – But she was more than that, you see?

She said I am the actress which allowed me to "mask truth as it sometimes happened to me." And the misconception that she is gone, is one of those masks, you see? She said, "I am the mother energy." And because energy is cosmic – it will always ever be. She called herself Mz.Conception and I think I understand why. Cosmic energy always exist in the universe and never can it die.

She said , "I am the fire-tender, the seer with third-eye sights. I am victorious in all challenges. I am the fight!" So how can she be truly gone, while the fire still brightly burns, the victory still is living, and the fight still struggles on?" It's a grave misconception, to think

that she is gone. For it is only the flesh that dies.
Strong spirits always live on.

She said, "I am the writer of what has been written."
She spoke of her pain and how tragedy had bitten. Yet
she triumphed in saying, she is "a survivor of having no
wings having flown" – but learned that her parchment
and her ink were her home. I find comfort in knowing
she found refuge in a thing with which I relate. For she
is an extraordinary poet. There is no doubt, nor debate.

There are realities on earth that are false or are true. But
it is no misconception, Connie, that friends and family
love you. It is no misconception that we poets love
you! It is no misconception P.O.E.T. adores you. It is
no misconception that you will be missed, for with each
word that we write, know that you have been kissed.

So peace to you, Connie, and although we cry, when we
see birds in flights in God's azure blue sky, we'll know
that you live, and that _you_ did not die. It's a cliché to
say, life changes in the twinkling of an eye. And it's
hard for us who love you to simply not cry. But in our
humble obedience, we do not question God why. But
thank Him for allowing your beautiful spirit to pass by.

ONE LITTLE THING

Before this Earth, I could not see –
and darkness everywhere covered me.
I was not physically blind nor in a tomb.
 I was simply in my mother's womb.
Upon this Earth, I could not see,
although light was now part of my memory
But I was young and was born free
and I felt the world was made for me.
I had no interest in other's plight
 – felt hunger, disease were not my fight.
If nations waged wars, what did I care?
 For national disasters were not my affair.
As I grew older, I still was blind.
 The only thing on Earth I wanted to find
Was fun, and enjoyment - just total pleasure.
 Doing nothing was my greatest treasure.
As I grew older still, my feelings grew worse.
 I was concerned only with the wealth in my purse.
And was there anything, in everything, for me.
 And nothing else on Earth could my eyes see.
But then one day, something came over me.
 I looked and I could see across the sea.
Where children were dying from lack of food.
Where rulers ruled with impunity and there were no rules.
I saw famine, diseases, sexual abuse –
 where degenerates used children for their sexual use.

Where families sold babies because they were poor
 and drug addiction did nothing but soar.
I saw hatred and bitterness between different races,
and shootings by police that in many cases
Were nothing but murder, just excuses to kill,
unarmed black men as though it gave them a thrill.
I saw cursing and cheating, and lying and stealing,
and grown folk who were perfectly, perfectly willing
To kill one another without a real reason,
as though death was just part of an open-sport season.
I turned from the waters and looked over here.
 What I saw only confirmed my greatest fear.
For all the atrocities I saw over there,
were tripled, in comparison, over here!
I was old now, yet now I could see,
 and what I saw completely devastated me.
And I cried out to God, "God, please help me –
Understand why all those years I could not see.
I have squandered money and fortune and time,
 and my indifference to others was simply a crime.
I don't know why I was so young and so blind.
 And why in my old age I suddenly find
That I could have done something to ease
the pain of suffering children. What can I do?
And God said, "The answer is inside of you.
  Yes, the years have passed and you have been blind.
But you have opened your eyes and now you can find,
 a way to make up – a way to repent
For all the foolish time on Earth you spent.
 Can you do one good deed?
Can you help one hungry child?
Can you hold one little baby who is wracked with pain?

Can you go to an asylum and help the insane?
Can you go to one nursing home
and help someone pray?
Someone whose speech has gone away?
Can you do one little thing
to aid one human being?
Can you say one kind word to someone
whose life has been tough?
And, my dear, that one little thing will be enough.
Just think if the millions of people on Earth.
All did one little thing.
What would it be worth?
There'd be million upon millions
 of kind little acts
And millions and millions
of folk would react
 to the one little thing
that has made their life better.
Can you clean oil from the wings
 – from the feathers?
Of a bird who unwittingly
rested on unclean waters?
It does not have to be a human
 you are kind to.
Animals, birds, even fish will do.
Do one little thing
for just one of my creatures.
Do one little thing, each day.
That is all that I ask.
And for your earlier blindness
I won't take you to task.
For it is only how today you live.
 For your past blindness

I will truly forgive
For past transgressions, I do understand.
 After all, I created you as only a man.
But if you do one little thing
of kindness each day, you see.
What you are saying in essence,
is that you believe in Me.
And your belief in Me will set you free,
and insure your heavenly eternity.
Again, it is what you do *today,*
that will determine your future, and decide which way
You will eventually end your Earthly stay.
 For I will open My arms as you come My way."

ABOUT THE AUTHOR

Loretta A. Hawkins is an American playwright, poet, author, social activist, spoken-word artist, and retired educator. Born in Winston-Salem, North Carolina, she grew up on the west side of Chicago, Illinois. She has earned five college degrees from Chicago City Colleges, Illinois Teachers College, Governors State University and The University of Chicago. After having taught school for thirty-four years, at every academic level, she reinvented herself as a spoken-word artist. She is the creator of four full-length plays, two educational workbooks, three children's books, a novel, a book of short fiction, essays and her work has been published or cited internationally. Hawkins' work, of various literary genres, have appeared in the following publications: *African Literature Today, Teaching Today, Major Poets, Individual Psychology Reporter, The University of Chicago Magazine, and Education Week*, among many others. She has won awards in all major genres. In 2016, she was awarded a Lifetime Achievement Award from the National Poetry Awards Society. Her first cd, *Only One Thing*, was awarded the Best Spoken Word CD of 2017. Her poetic name is Firekeeper, and she is a member of P.O.E.T. Inc. (People Of Extraordinary Talent.)

www.ingramcontent.com/pod-product-compliance
Lightning Source LLC
Chambersburg PA
CBHW032059040426
42449CB00007B/1141